# He is looking for his oil lamp.

It is dark in the attic.

Grandad and Quentin have still not found the oil lamp.

Scarlett has found the oil lamp!

er  Ue
ou  Oi
ue  Er
ar  Qu
oi  Ou
qu  Ar

I  the

This is Mervin.

This is Mervin's garden.

- boots
- a fork
- soil
- a squirrel
- a statue

In his garden, Mervin has carrots, beetroot, radishes, parsnips…

'Get off!' shouts Mervin.

| | |
|---|---|
| oi | Qu |
| qu | Ue |
| er | Er |
| ar | Ar |
| ou | Oi |
| ue | Ou |

she  he

Mark is a spoilsport.

He spoils his sister's fun.

Mark whizzes along.

# He speeds around the corner...

...and lands in the duck pond!

# Dad rescues Mark from the pond.

Mark shivers on a park bench.